NEW NEGRO POETS U.S.A.

EDITED BY LANGSTON HUGHES

NEW

NEGRO

POETS

U. S. A.

FOREWORD BY GWENDOLYN BROOKS

Indiana University Press
Bloomington & London

To Larry and Margaret

ACKNOWLEDGMENTS

Acknowledgment is made to the following poets and publications for permission to reprint the poems in this volume: Robert J. Abrams for "Two Poems," Samuel Allen for "Love Song" and "If the Stars Should Fall," Vivian Ayers for "Instantaneous," Lerone Bennett for "Blues and Bitterness," Julian Bond for "Rotation" and "Habana," Helen Morgan Brooks for "Words" and "Plans," Isabella Brown for "Prayer," Margaret Danner for "Garnishing the Aviary," "Dance of the Abakweta," and "Visit of the Professor," Thomas Dent for "Love" and "Come Visit My Garden," Ray Durem for "Award," James A. Emanuel for "Wedding Procession," "The Voyage of Jimmy Poo" (© 1961 by the New York Times Company and reprinted by permission), and "The Treehouse" (© 1961 by Phylon and reprinted by permission), Julia Fields for "Madness One Monday Evening" and "I Heard a Young Man Saying," Carl Gardner for "Reflections," David Henderson for "Sketches of Harlem" and "Downtown-Boy Uptown," Calvin C. Hernton for "The Distant Drum" and "Madhouse," Don Johnson for "O White Mistress," LeRoi Jones for "Lines to Garcia Lorca" (reprinted from Yugen, with the author's permission), "Epistrophe" (reprinted from The Beat Scene, Corinth Books, New York, with the author's permission), "Preface to a Twenty Volume Suicide Note" (Totem/Corinth, New York, with the author's permission), and "Each Morning," Audre G. Lorde for "And Fall Shall Sit in Judgment" and "Pirouette," Naomi Long Madgett for "Midway" (first published in Freedomways, Fall, 1961) and "Mortality," Gloria C. Oden for "The Map," "Review From Staten Island," and "A Private Letter to Brazil," Raymond Patterson for "When I Awoke," Oliver Pitcher for "The

ACKNOWLEDGMENTS

Pale Blue Casket" and "Raison d'Etre" (from the poem "Jean-Jacques" published in *Dust of Silence* by the Troubador Press), Dudley Randall for "Legacy: My South," "The Southern Road," and "Memorial Wreath," Thurmond Snyder for "Beale Street, "The Beast," and "Seeds," James Vaughn for "Three Kings," "Movie Queen," and "Two Ladies Bidding Us 'Good Morning'," and Mance Williams for "Lover Man and . . ." and "A Year Without Seasons."

CONTENTS

Foreword 13

I

This Morning   Jay Wright   17
Love Song   Samuel Allen   18
Point of No Return   Mari Evans   19
And Fall Shall Sit in Judgment   Audre Lorde   20
The Treehouse   James A. Emanuel   21
If There Be Sorrow   Mari Evans   22
Mortality   Naomi Long Madgett   23
Three Kings   James P. Vaughn   24

II

Far from Africa   Margaret Danner   29
Award   Ray Durem   33
It Is Time   Ted Joans   34
My America   Oliver La Grone   36
This Hour   Oliver La Grone   37
Bathed Is My Blood   Oliver La Grone   38
Midway   Naomi Long Madgett   39
O White Mistress   Don Johnson   40
The Southern Road   Dudley Randall   41
On Passing Two Negroes . . .   Conrad Kent Rivers   42
Legacy: My South   Dudley Randall   43
The Still Voice of Harlem   Conrad Kent Rivers   44
Face of Poverty   Lucy Smith   45
The Map   G. C. Oden   47

CONTENTS

III

Blues and Bitterness	*Lerone Bennett*	53
Beale Street, Memphis	*Thurmond Snyder*	54
Lines to Garcia Lorca	*LeRoi Jones*	55
For Lover Man, and All the Other Young Men Who Failed to Return from World War II	*Mance Williams*	56
John Coltrane—An Impartial Review	*Alfred B. Spellman*	57
The Citizen	*Vilma Howard*	58
Memorial Wreath	*Dudley Randall*	59
Zapata & the Landlord	*Alfred B. Spellman*	60
Prayer	*Isabella M. Brown*	61
Movie Queen	*James P. Vaughn*	62
Two Ladies Bidding Us "Good Morning"	*James P. Vaughn*	63

IV

Rotation	*Julian Bond*	67
A Year Without Seasons	*Mance Williams*	68
The Noonday April Sun	*George Love*	69
Brothers	*Solomon Edwards*	70
Love	*Tom Dent*	71
Stopped	*Allen Polite*	72
Epistrophe	*LeRoi Jones*	73
Each Morning	*LeRoi Jones*	74
Dream	*Solomon Edwards*	75
Sketches of Harlem	*David Henderson*	76
Shrine To What Should Be	*Mari Evans*	77
Madness One Monday Evening	*Julia Fields*	78
. . . and the old women gathered	*Mari Evans*	79
Come Visit My Garden	*Tom Dent*	80
Wedding Procession	*James A. Emanuel*	81
Shoplifter	*Solomon Edwards*	82
The .38	*Ted Joans*	83
Instantaneous	*Vivian Ayers*	85
Habana	*Julian Bond*	86

CONTENTS

The Beast with Chrome Teeth   *Thurmond Snyder*   87
Seeds   *Thurmond Snyder*   88
Review from Staten Island   *G. C. Oden*   90
A Private Letter to Brazil   *G. C. Oden*   91

V

If the Stars Should Fall   *Samuel Allen*   95
Preface to a Twenty Volume
    Suicide Note   *LeRoi Jones*   96
The Voyage of Jimmy Poo   *James A. Emanuel*   97
Reflections   *Carl Gardner*   98
Downtown-Boy Uptown   *David Henderson*   99
The Distant Drum   *Calvin C. Hernton*   101
Madhouse   *Calvin C. Hernton*   102
Am Driven Mad   *Allen Polite*   103
Words   *Helen Morgan Brooks*   104
Where Have You Gone . . . ?   *Mari Evans*   105
Pirouette   *Audre Lorde*   106
Four sheets to the wind and a
    one-way ticket to France   *Conrad Kent Rivers*   107
Plans   *Helen Morgan Brooks*   109
I Heard a Young Man Saying   *Julia Fields*   110
Two Poems   *Robert J. Abrams*   111
When I Awoke   *Raymond Patterson*   113
The Pale Blue Casket   *Oliver Pitcher*   114
Raison d'Etre   *Oliver Pitcher*   115

Biographical Notes   117

Index of Names   127

FOREWORD

At the present time, poets who happen also to be Negroes are twice-tried. They have to write poetry, and they have to remember that they are Negroes. Often they wish that they could solve the Negro question once and for all, and go on from such success to the composition of textured sonnets or buoyant villanelles about the transience of a raindrop, or the gold-stuff of the sun. *They* are likely to find significances in those subjects not instantly obvious to their fairer fellows. The raindrop may seem to them to represent racial tears—and those might seem, indeed, other than transient. The golden sun might remind them that they are burning.

In the work of most of today's Negro poets the reader will discover evidences of double dedication, hints that the artists have accepted a two-headed responsibility. Few have favored a trek without flags or emblems of any racial kind; and even those few, in their deliberate "renunciation," have in effect spoken racially, have offered race-fed testimony of several sorts.

In 1950 I remarked in *Phylon,* "Every Negro poet has 'something to say.' Simply because he is a Negro, he cannot escape having important things to say. His mere body, for that matter, is an eloquence. His quiet walk down the street is a speech to the people. Is a rebuke, is a plea, is a school. But no real artist is going to be content with offering raw materials." This is as true today—when we, white and black, are a collective pregnancy that is going to proceed to its inevitability, getting worse before it gets better—as it was before the major flower of the volcano.

New Negro Poets: U.S.A. is officially divided into five parts—"lyrical, protest, personal and general descriptions, and personal,

13

reflective statements." The interests overlap, of course, at many points. But on any page the reader is apt to notice passion, or a desperate comedy, or an adult anger which may be intellectual or intestinal, or a wishful joy. He may sight lightning, working through the mesh of a seemingly becalmed body of meditation.

The large triumph here is the realization on the part of the majority of these poets that no matter how important are their informing truths, *poetry* is to be the result of their involvement with emotion and idea and pen and paper. Success is not the reward of every effort. But there is enough magic, enough sure flight, enough meaningful strength to inspire a happy surmise that here are some of the prevailing stars of an early tomorrow.

GWENDOLYN BROOKS

NEW NEGRO POETS U.S.A.

I

THIS MORNING

Jay Wright

This morning I threw the windows
of my room open, the light burst
in like crystal gauze and I hung
it on my wall to frame.
And here I am watching it take possession
of my room, watching the obscure love
match of light and shadow—of cold and warmth.
It is a matter of acceptance, I guess.
It is a matter of finding some room
with shadows to embrace, open. Now
the light has settled in, I don't think
I shall ever close my windows again.

LOVE SONG

Samuel Allen

An arrow rides upon the sky,
It does not pause or ask the way.
It rides the sweet and evening sky,
It bursts upon its startled prey.

A driving shaft, hermetic heart,
Love split the guardian hate
With scorn that only eyes impart
Should she retaliate.

Now beauty hides a vandal's face.
Yours stripped my tall heart bare,
Still hell is an entrancing place
Because you're going there.

POINT OF NO RETURN

Mari Evans

You say yes and I say yes
. . . . alas
and then we walk together yes
. . . . alas
then you say no and I say please
. . . . alas
then I say no and you agree
. . . . alas
then you return to plead a plea
. . . . alas
but oh so late oh much
. . . . too late
. . . . alas

AND FALL SHALL SIT
IN JUDGMENT

Audre Lorde

Through the long winter
harshly, fairly
we judged our love.
But spring came early.

Winter's white quiet
trusting, steady
birthed sudden fury—
and we were not ready.

Distraught with spring
and the earth's wild greening
we gave our love
a false new meaning—

Who suffered to learn
when the autumn came
that love in all seasons
is false, but the same.

THE TREEHOUSE

James A. Emanuel

To every man
His treehouse,
A green splice in the humping years,
Spartan with narrow cot
And prickly door.

To every man
His twilight flash
Of luminous recall
   of tiptoe years
   in leaf-stung flight;
   of days of squirm and bite
   that waved antennas through the grass;
   of nights
   when every moving thing
   was girlshaped,
   expectantly turning.

To every man
His house below
And his house above—
With perilous stairs
Between.

IF THERE BE SORROW

Mari Evans

If there be sorrow
let it be
for things undone . . .
undreamed
  unrealized
    unattained
to these add one:
Love withheld . . .
. . . restrained

MORTALITY

Naomi Long Madgett

This is the surest death
Of all the deaths I know.
The one that halts the breath,
The one that falls with snow
Are nothing but a peace
Before the second zone,
For Aprils never cease
To resurrect their own,
And in my very veins
Flows blood as old as Eve.
The smallest cell contains
Its privileged reprieve.
But vultures recognize
This single mortal thing
And watch with hungry eyes
When hope starts staggering.

THREE KINGS

James P. Vaughn

Three kings went down to the soul of the sea
            to counsel with their elders.
Three kings went down
        breathlessly
        down to the bole of the sea
These three kings
           Arius   Darius   Marius
    Down went
               Arius
               limping
               through the crystalshade
                   the grottoglade
                   the always murmuring sea

                   "Poor King Arius"
                   sighed Darius and Marius
                   in the whispermist of the warm sandshore
                   "it seems he'll never return"

Two kings gazed with gravity
into the hole of the smothering sea
"who will it be   who will it be
to go to counsel with the elders"   "oh,
              let me
              let me
              let me

              go"
              asked Darius
              emboldened
                   to wade the nefarious jade of the sea

Down went
     Darius
     delicately
     into the mold of the
     silence   silence
     the always silence, the always gathering sea

          never to return
          with the fathers' fiat

Now
     stands precarious
     the lonely Marius

          before the knell of the rising sea

Quietly   Quietly   Quietly

II

FAR FROM AFRICA

Margaret Danner

"are you beautiful still?"

1.

Garnishing the Aviary

Our molting days are in their twilight stage.
These lengthy dreaded suns of draggling plumes.
These days of moods that swiftly alternate between

The former preen (ludicrous now) and a downcast rage
Or crest-fallen lag, are fading out. The initial bloom;
Exotic, dazzling in its indigo, tangerine

Splendor; this rare, conflicting coat had to be shed.
Our drooping feathers turn all shades. We spew
This unamicable aviary, gag upon the worm, and fling

Our loosening quills. We make a riotous spread
Upon the dust and mire that beds us. We do not shoo
So quickly; but the shades of the pinfeathers resulting

From this chaotic push, though still exotic,
Blend more easily with those on the wings
Of the birds surrounding them; garnishing
The aviary, burnishing this zoo.

Dance of the Abakweta

Imagine what Mrs. Haessler would say
If she could see the Watussi youth dance
Their well-versed initiation. At first glance
As they bend to an invisible barre
You would know that she had designed their costumes.

For though they were made of pale beige bamboo straw
Their lines were the classic tutu. Nothing varied.
Each was cut short to the thigh and carried
High to a degree of right angles. Nor was there a flaw
In their leotards. Made of leopard skin or the hide

Of a goat, or the Gauguin-colored Okapi's striped coat
They were cut in her reverenced "tradition."
She would have approved their costumes and positions.
And since neither Iceland nor Africa is too remote
For her vision she would have wanted to form

A "traditional" ballet. Swan Lake, Scheherazade or
(After seeing their incredible leaps)
Les Orientales. Imagine the exotic sweep
Of such a ballet, and from the way the music pours
Over these dancers (this tinkling of bells, talking

Of drums, and twanging of tan, sandalwood harps)
From this incomparable music, Mrs. Haessler of Vassar can
Glimpse strains of Tchaikovsky, Chopin
To accompany her undeviatingly sharp
"Traditional" ballet. I am certain that if she could
Tutor these potential protégés, as
Quick as Aladdin rubbing his lamp, she would.

3.

The Visit of the Professor of Aesthetics

To see you standing in the sagging bookstore door
So filled me with chagrin that suddenly you seemed as
Pink and white to me as a newborn, hairless mouse. For

I had hoped to delight you at home. Be a furl
Of faint perfume and Vienna's cord-like lace.
To shine my piano till a shimmer of mother-of-pearl

Embraced it. To pleasantly surprise you with the grace
That transcends by imitation and much worn
"Louis XV" couch. To display my cathedrals and ballets.

To plunge you into Africa through my nude
Zulu Prince, my carvings from Benin, forlorn
Treasures garnered by much sacrifice of food.

I had hoped to delight you, for more
Rare than the seven-year bloom of my
Chinese spiderweb fern is a mind like yours

That concedes my fetish for this substance
Of your trade. And I had planned to prove
Your views of me correct at even every chance

Encounter. But you surprised me. And the store which
Had shown promise until you came, arose
Like a child gone wild when company comes or a witch

At Hallowe'en. The floor, just swept and mopped
Was persuaded by the northlight to deny it.
The muddy rag floor rugs hunched and flopped

Away from the tears in the linoleum that I wanted
Them to hide. The drapes that I had pleated
In clear orchid and peach feverishly flaunted

Their greasiest folds like a banner.
The books who had been my friends, retreated—
Became as shy as the proverbial poet in manner

And hid their better selves. All glow had been deleted
By the dirt. And I felt that you whose god is grace
Could find no semblance of it here. And unaware

That you were scrubbing, you scrubbed your hands.
Wrung and scrubbed your long white fingers. Scrubbed
Them as you smiled and I lowered my eyes from despair.

AWARD

Ray Durem

*A Gold Watch to the FBI
Man who has followed
me for 25 Years.*

Well, old spy
looks like I
led you down some pretty blind alleys,
took you on several trips to Mexico,
fishing in the high Sierras,
jazz at the Philharmonic.
You've watched me all your life,
I've clothed your wife,
put your two sons through college.
what good has it done?
the sun keeps rising every morning.
ever see me buy an Assistant President?
or close a school?
or lend money to Trujillo?
ever catch me rigging airplane prices?
I bought some after-hours whiskey in L.A.
but the Chief got his pay.
I ain't killed no Koreans
or fourteen-year-old boys in Mississippi.
neither did I bomb Guatemala,
or lend guns to shoot Algerians.
I admit I took a Negro child
to a white rest room in Texas,
but she was my daughter, only three,
who had to pee.

IT IS TIME

Ted Joans

It is time for the United States to spend money on education so
  that every American would be hipper, *thus no war!*

It is time for the garbage men to treat garbage cans as they treat
  their mothers

It is time for the Union of the Soviet Socialist Republics to raise
  the Iron Curtain and let the world dig 'em ?

It is time for all museums of art to stop charging admission fees

It is time for the electric chair to give birth to an electric couch
  thus enabling the entire family to go together *Cross sign*

It is time for Madison Avenue to tell the truth and nothing but
  the truth so help them Mr. Clean

It is time for square jivey leaguers to stop saying 'he's sick, she's
  sick, they're sick, sick sick sick'

It is time for the Brooklyn bridge to fall on a boat load of DAR
  fair ladies ?

It is time for the races of the world to ball and ball and ball and
  then there will be no reason for war at all

It is time for the Statue of Liberty to be replaced by a Statue of
  Uncle Tom

It is time for the Post Office to employ only the blind to sort out
  the mail

It is time for the police headquarters to share their building with
  young nuns

34

It is time for Steve Allen to be the next president of the United States, Dizzy Gillespie Sec of State and Kim Novak our Minister of Foreign Affairs

It is time for jazz and more jazz and some more jazz and still some more jazz

It is time for the American Indians to be made multimillionaires

It is time for the keys to be left in the mail box again

It is time for rhinoceroses to roam the streets of Little Rock and spread joy

It is time for a moral revolution in America

It is time for the world to love and Love and LOVE

It is time for everybody to swing (Life don't mean a thing if it don't swing) yes that is right because

It's time it is time to straighten up and fly right tonight

35

MY AMERICA

Oliver La Grone

O mongrel land!
O patchworked quilt of bloods!
Samplings of earth tracked to and fro,
What is your promise?

O homeland!
Land of my second birth,
And other births to come,
See here!
My countenance,
Bearing the look
Of myriad eyes,
Mouthing all tales of men.
See here, my searching, seeking . . .
I am the digger in your depths,—
Finder and bringer of this
Crude stone of fire . . .
This polished piece is faceted,
Each face a fire-eye for your rainbow lustre.
This is my gift to you from out these deeps,
Where also I found fool's gold . . .
Now I bring aloft chilled
Hands; the gem as yet, is
Lukewarm to the blood . . .

THIS HOUR
(WRITTEN AFTER WAR)

Oliver La Grone

In this the hour of new reckonings!
In this the hour when men pray for dawn—
When bayonet and barbed wire
Guard the steps,
And all the blood banks drain . . .
In this the hour when
Freedom's promise is
Torn and hacked
To waver in the wind—
And piled high at its feet
The carnage, dross,
And dung
Of all the passions—
And worms and fishes
Gather for the feast—
In this the hour
When the planners meet,
Hear!
Lest greedy men set bargaining
Again,
O planners hear!
My speech is simple,
You read it from the footfalls
Of my past.
It is my blood!
My hands!
My body!
Seeding deep across these ways.
It is my buried tongues of hope—
Struck dumb by fire and
Drowned in lifeless sod—
Still crying out for life!!

BATHED IS MY BLOOD

Oliver La Grone

Bathed is my blood
In the many dawns that passed.
The quest of newborn light
Fevers the stream
Where lives and flowers
My timeless dream.

Old East, New West,
The paling lairs of polar light,
The tropic fire mirage,
These heard my heart's
Eternal chants . . .

Before my eyes the crested moon,
The myriad teat points
On the breast of night
Have weaned a morning
Star above the pyramids
And crossed the manger's door
With light,
In argosies to shores of dawn.

MIDWAY

Naomi Long Madgett

I've come this far to freedom
And I won't turn back.
I'm climbing to the highway
From my old dirt track.
I'm coming and I'm going
And I'm stretching and I'm growing
And I'll reap what I've been sowing
Or my skin's not black.
I've prayed and slaved and waited
And I've sung my song.
You've bled me and you've starved me
But I've still grown strong.
You've lashed me and you've treed me
And you've everything but freed me,
But in time you'll know you need me
And it won't be long.
I've seen the daylight breaking
High above the bough.
I've found my destination and I've made my vow;
So whether you abhor me
Or deride me or ignore me,
Mighty mountains loom before me
And I won't stop now.

O WHITE MISTRESS

Don Johnson

O White Mistress,
O tangible feeling of superiority,
Stand if you wish
But your child is sleepy
Lay him next to me and I
Will give him warmth. Poor soul,
      Wretched existence, vain life,
O egoism, pride, Southern mores,
O indoctrinated cattle of an illusion.

THE SOUTHERN ROAD

Dudley Randall

There the black river, boundary to hell,
And here the iron bridge, the ancient car,
And grim conductor, who with surly yell
Forbids white soldiers where the black ones are.
And I re-live the enforced avatar
Of desperate journey to a dark abode
Made by my sires before another war;
And I set forth upon the southern road.

To a land where shadowed songs like flowers swell
And where the earth is scarlet as a scar
Friezed by the bleeding lash that fell (O fell!)
Upon my fathers' flesh. O far, far, far
And deep my blood has drenched it. None can bar
My birthright to the loveliness bestowed
Upon this country haughty as a star.
And I set forth upon the southern road.

This darkness and these mountains loom a spell
Of peak-roofed town where yearning steeples soar
And the holy holy chanting of a bell
Shakes human incense on the throbbing air
Where bonfires blaze and quivering bodies char.
Whose is the hair that crisped, and fiercely glowed?
I know it; and my entrails melt like tar
And I set forth upon the southern road.

O fertile hillsides where my fathers are,
And whence my woes like troubled streams have flowed,
Love you I must, though they may sweep me far.
And I set forth upon the southern road.

ON PASSING TWO NEGROES
ON A DARK COUNTRY ROAD
SOMEWHERE IN GEORGIA

Conrad Kent Rivers

This road is like a tomb
Carrying souls to stranger realms.
A broken face, patched pants, moonlight,
Late dinner and sleep in a crowded room.
Let us hope that our gods dance
And eat cornbread from a wooden spoon,
When night enters
With a cool breeze
To sooth an aching back.

LEGACY: MY SOUTH

Dudley Randall

What desperate nightmare rapts me to this land
Lit by a bloody moon, red on the hills,
Red in the valleys? Why am I compelled
To tread again where buried feet have trod,
To shed my tears where blood and tears have flowed?
Compulsion of the blood and of the moon
Transports me. I was molded from this clay.
My blood must ransom all the blood shed here,
My tears redeem the tears. Cripples and monsters
Are here. My flesh must make them whole and hale.
I am the sacrifice.

           See where the halt
Attempt again and again to cross a line
Their minds have drawn, but fear snatches them back
Though health and joy wait on the other side.
And there another locks himself in a room
And throws away the key. A ragged scarecrow
Cackles an antique lay, and cries himself
Lord of the world. A naked plowman falls
Famished upon the plow, and overhead
A lean bird circles.

THE STILL VOICE OF HARLEM

Conrad Kent Rivers

Come to me broken dreams and all
      bring me the glory of fruitless souls,
I shall find a place for them in my gardens.

Weep not for the golden sun of California,
      think not of the fertile soil of Alabama . . .
nor your father's eyes, your mother's body twisted
      by the washing board.

I am the hope of your unborn,
      truly, when there is no more of me . . .
there shall be no more of you. . . .

FACE OF POVERTY

Lucy Smith

No one can communicate to you
The substance of poverty—
Can tell you either the shape,
        or the depth,
                or the breadth
Of poverty—
Until you have lived with her intimately.

No one can guide your fingers
Over the rims of her eye sockets,
Over her hollow cheeks—
Until perhaps one day
In your wife's once pretty face
You see the lines of poverty;
Until you feel
In her now skinny body,
The protruding bones,
The barely covered ribs,
The shrunken breasts of poverty,

Poverty can be a stranger
In a far-off land:
An alien face
Briefly glimpsed in a newsreel,
An empty rice bowl
In a skinny brown hand,
Until one bleak day
You look out the window—
And poverty is the squatter
In your own backyard.

Poverty wails in the night for milk,
Not knowing the price of a quart.

It is desperation in your teen-ager's face,
Wanting a new evening gown for the junior prom,
After going through school in rummage store clothes.
It is a glass of forgetfulness sold over the bar.

And poverty's voice is a jeer in the night—
       "You may bring another child
       Into the rat race that is your life;
       You may cut down on food
       To buy contraceptives;
       You may see your wife walk alone
       Down some back alley route
       To a reluctant appointment
       With an unsterile knife—
       Or you may sleep alone."
And one morning shaving
You look in the mirror—
And never again will poverty be alien,
For the face of poverty is not over your shoulder,
The face of poverty is your own.
And hearing the break in your wife's voice
At the end of a bedtime story,
You realize that somewhere along the way
The stock ending in your own story went wrong.
And now you no longer ask
That you and your wife
Will live happily ever after—
But simply that you
And your wife
And your children
Will live.

THE MAP

G. C. Oden

My rug is red. My couch, whereon I deal
in dreams with truths I never live, is brown;
a shading more intense than that by my
skin declared. Richer it is, too, than of
any of the eight clear hues coloring
my wide, world map soldiering the white wall
there behind it. This map is of the world.
It says so. In type ½" high: WORLD;
and with what I know of maps I do, indeed, believe it—though over it, in type
now smaller by one-half, I read the word
"COSMOPOLITAN," and over that, in
type yet smaller by one-half, these gentle
modifiers "RAND McNALLY."

                                      The seas
square off in blue. Or, ought the word be "sea"?
Uniformly bright, planed by a tone so
mild you might suppose the North Sea twinned the
South and that the Moskenstraumen was (for
the most part) Poe (quote) *Sailing directions
for the northwest and north coast of Norway*
(unquote) to the contrary; seven diminishes
to one, where none arrests attention.

                                      Not
so the land. Flowering forth as spring in
May will settle down to deed, it woos us
with such yellows, pinks and greens as would, I'm
sure, lure the most selective butterfly;
and each trim hue is sized the living room
of nations.

America (U.S.) is
daffodil; Canada carnation; while
leaf-like as an elephant ear, Greenland
hangs indifferent to those arctic winds parching
the cell-like bounds of Russia (here halved and
showing both to the left and right of this
our hemisphere—indeed, as is a good
part of the orient split, some even
to doubling appearance.)

Europe (also)
lies fragmented; though from nature's—not the
mapmaker's—division. Ireland off-
set from England, offset from France (feigning
oasis beside the rot-brown fill to
Germany) supplies one awkward revel
of abstraction as that gross bud of Spain
(with Portugal) patterns another; not
to mention Italy's invasion of
the sea.

Norway, Sweden, much as giraffes
must bend, towards Denmark group in restricted
convenant; yet, though this canvas—Europe—
at its center holds, such unity rests
more upon imagination than that,
let's say of Africa islanded in
those deeper latitudes.

There, it is the
green (again) I think. In candescent flood
like the dead reckoning of spring; at four
points edging sea; it seems a fever of
the mind within that broad head housed (it shapes
—Africa—a head to me!) which in its
course will blaze the length of continent as
now it fires breadth.

And who will say it
won't? Not the mapmaker, surely, who must
exact truth. Not I, high hoisting same to
state whirlwind. Will you, because you might not
particularly care to see it so?

III

BLUES AND BITTERNESS

(FOR BILLIE HOLIDAY)

Lerone Bennett

Ice tinkled in glasses,
froze and rolled away
from hearts
in tombs where she slept.
Smoke noosed,
coiled and dangled from ceilings
in caves where she wept.

I woke up this morning
Just befo' the break of day.
I was bitter, blue and black, Lawd.
There ain't nothing else to say.

In saloons
festooned with trumpets
she prayed—sang
love songs to dead men
waiting with hammers
at the bottom of syringes.
She sang it in a song
before Sartre put it into a book.
She was Bigger
before Wright wrote,
was with Nekeela
in a slave coffle,
was stripped, branded
and eaten by the sharks
and rose again
on the third day in Georgia.

I wondered why God made me.
I wondered why He made me black.
I wondered why Mama begat me—
And I started to give God His ticket back.

BEALE STREET, MEMPHIS

Thurmond Snyder

Neon glitter of night
Rain splatters quietly
Silhouettes, shadows
Estranged from corporeal existence

Poltergeists ramble
Among ruins
A corpse lies lonely
In an alley coffin

Out of a dark street
Into a brilliant vertigo of sound
A mask falls
A player leaves the stage

Guatama has returned
From the mountain
The naked eye of truth
Bears the stain of a lonely tear.

LINES TO GARCIA LORCA

LeRoi Jones

> *Climin up the mountin, chillun,*
> *Didn't come here for to stay,*
> *If I'm ever gonna see you agin,*
> *It'll be on the judgment day.*
>   *—Negro Spiritual*

Send soldiers again to kill you, Garcia.
Send them to quell my escape.
These things mean nothing.
You are dying again, Garcia.
This is all I remember.
Send soldiers again, Garcia.
Hail Mary,
Holy mother,
Pray for me.

I live near a mountain, green mirror
Of burning paths and a low sun
To measure my growing by.
There is a wind that repeats
A bird's name and near his
Cage is a poem, and a small boy herding
Cattle with diamonds
In their mouths.

Mandolins grow on the high slopes
And orange-robed monks collect songs
Just beyond the last line of fruit trees.
Naked girls pretend they are butterflies,
And a deer tells stories to the twilight.

Garcia, where is my Bible?
I want to read those myths
Again.   No answer.
But, away off, quite close to the daylight,
I hear his voice, and he is laughing, laughing
Like a Spanish guitar.

FOR LOVER MAN, AND ALL THE OTHER YOUNG MEN WHO FAILED TO RETURN FROM WORLD WAR II

Mance Williams

Like so many other young men in those troubled
years, you abandoned your youth and your identity;
and you left the corners, the women, and the jazz
behind; and you reluctantly exchanged your three

button roll for a drab without class; then you
hurried to catch the last set at Minton's.
Bird was there and you wondered if he knew exactly
what he was trying to do; then you left—without a

kiss for Billie—for a place you had never heard of
nor ever cared existed; and there you lived with
more danger than you had ever encountered in the city.

Like so many of the young men in those troubled years,
you went away; and like so many of them you never came
back. And like so many other young hearts, Billie
was singing:
> *Oh lover man*
> *Oh where can you be?*

JOHN COLTRANE

AN IMPARTIAL REVIEW

Alfred B. Spellman

may he have new life like the fall
fallen tree, wet moist rotten enough
to see shoots stalks branches & green
leaves (& may the roots) grow into his side.

around the back of the mind, in its closet
is a string, i think, a coil around things.
listen to *summertime*, think of spring, negroes
cats in the closet, anything that makes a rock

of your eye. imagine you steal. you are frightened
you want help. you are sorry you are born with ears

THE CITIZEN

Vilma Howard

Wearing his equality like a too-small shoe,
which looks good
and modifies the foot,
measures himself in stories up
and escalators down,
suits tempo of the hoof
to iamb of the herd
plunging into the subway.

(Remembering to be creative,
buys a tree tamed into a desk,
paints a jail around the wood,
not seeing where—as the rings,
one after another,
mount into that corner—
a single nail hangs loose.)

Keeping in wide separation
the extremes of things, the horns
parenthesize the middle path.
The dilemma solved,
the solution thus contained,
the citizen
is soundly squared
without remainder or loose end,
and goes about as always,
full of the importance
of carrying briefcases.

MEMORIAL WREATH

Dudley Randall

(For the more than 200,000
Negroes who served in the Union
Army during the Civil War)

In this green month when resurrected flowers,
Like laughing children ignorant of death,
Brighten the couch of those who wake no more,
Love and remembrance blossom in our hearts
For you who bore the extreme sharp pang for us,
And bought our freedom with your lives.

And now,
Honoring your memory, with love we bring
These fiery roses, white-hot cotton flowers
And violets bluer than cool northern skies
You dreamed of in the burning prison fields
When liberty was only a faint north star,
Not a bright flower planted by your hands
Reaching up hardy nourished with your blood.

Fit gravefellows you are for Lincoln, Brown
And Douglass and Toussaint . . . all whose rapt eyes
Fashioned a new world in this wilderness.

American earth is richer for your bones;
Our hearts beat prouder for the blood we inherit.

ZAPATA & THE LANDLORD

Alfred B. Spellman

the thief in me is running a
round in circles. what will he
do? how will he
                fight an army?
hide somewhere, a shade
                        among shadows?
o the embarrassment, the tedium of coming
so far & failing.
                e.g., the mexican, emiliano
& anthony, touched
                by the thief, run off to the
mountains by the thief, returned with their 3000
brothers
        & brought back the mountain.
                                        well, i
have only one
                brother, roland, 18,
& he has never fought
                a thief.

PRABER

Isabella M. Brown

I had thought of putting an
altar here in the house,
just a small corner.
Anyway, I usually fall down on my knees
anywhere in the house.
I get on my knees and bow down
without thinking anything sometimes.
I say sometimes
God, here is my mind.
That's a good prayer
because during these times
there is almost always none.
So I ask God to hold my mind
and lead me in His path.

It sure is raining hard today.

MOVIE QUEEN

James P. Vaughn

                           she

wore
      her flossiest smile
      no enigma dare
      disturb her haven of paint, so she

faced
      the human camera;
      this is how
      my eye printed her when she

entered
      the hypothetical room
      rigged in innocence
      tough as her shag of silk, but when she

left
      I saw cracks
      in her elbows
      and the blonde bun (that went for the ride)

stuck
      at the foot of her head.

TWO LADIES BIDDING US "GOOD MORNING"

James P. Vaughn

I

Mrs. Hobart-Constantine awakens

adjusts her high
pink pompadour
in mime of mistresses
of Louis Sieze

contemplates
shoes for short patters
to and fro

completes the petty craft
of rouge and emollient

for steppings through the large outdoors

(in the mountains of Andalusia
a guitar string snaps—
breaking those midmorning fashionings)

slightly, very slightly
Mrs. Hobart-Constantine trembles

is as pale as statuary

but, oh! through this intermission
what brisk fingers repel impertinence
the bootsteps of years
stomping a consummation to
a minor war?

II

Miss Amanda Burr, always equivocal
arose that morning
emerging
as though out of the fancy
        of Botticelli—
lost in small crucibles
        she had no predominant theory
        no grand ideal to surge her on
at times—
                she heard and could not hear
                voices that passed her ear
                whose touch caressed her ghost?
she counted as least
the stark triangle of walls
that contained her notion of space
she fought her wars as Agamemnon had
alone
        the flutter of an eyelid
        composed a lifetime

                she imagined hooves
                crossing the Aqua Claudia
                approaching . . . passing
at 10 o'clock—
                a crown in her pannier
                Miss Amanda Burr
                goes out into the bright eclipse.

IV

ROTATION

Julian Bond

Like plump green floor plans
the pool tables squat
Among fawning mahogany Buddhas with felt heads.
Like clubwomen blessed with adultery
The balls dart to kiss
and tumble erring members into silent oblivion.
Right-angled over the verdant barbered turf
Sharks point long fingers at the multi-colored worlds
and play at percussion
Sounding cheap plastic clicks
in an 8-ball universe built for ivory.

A YEAR WITHOUT SEASONS

Mance Williams

This year (so I hear)
Will come and go all
In one breath. Days
Will have no futures
And will catch their
Past somewhere in space. A race
Without a winner.

A green Christmas without a winter.

An open door leads you
Into a damp musty throat
Where over in the corner
Beside a paneled larynx
An old dresser drawer contains
The unwritten epitaphs of an
Entire civilization.

You are the only survivor—
So don't speak. Do not even hum
Your favorite song. Strangulation
Could occur with one slip of the tongue.

THE NOONDAY APRIL SUN

George Love

when through the winding cobbled streets of time
new spring is borne upon the voices of young boys
when all around the grass grows up like laughter
and visions grow like grass beneath our feet
then roads run out like wine
and eyes like tongues drink up the streams of longing

o then remembrance rages at the tyranny of days
and men within their shabby inward rooms
get up to press their faces to the windowpanes
and then run down in rivers to the sea of dreams

BROTHERS

Solomon Edwards

They grew and charcoal bundle shakes itself,
Surprises: comes to rapid feet and fur.
For me his stare of green is standard gulf
Until his mother and his brother share
A welcome. I surmise which paw to shake,
And two, then four are nestled in my care.

Discover Cricket, carbon-silk and sleek,
Whose silver forenails dart and search my lap;
He nods to brother Murray's noiseless trek
And follows grace which ends his perfect leap
Beside us. Back upright, hind legs a base,
He seems a banker dined, who—yes, will tip.

No Corsican or Karamazov, these
Are brothers led by a simpler, finer mood;
They like to milk and cuddle, may climb trees.
To keep their mother's blondness gay is food.

LOVE

Tom Dent

the gold of heaven
the blue of hell
the sun of day
the tomb of night—
the golden sun
anchoring my
spinning heart
while a blue tomb
lurks icily in
the dark.

STOPPED

Allen Polite

Everything is stopped
Stopped as the table is stopped
Sand without wind
   the still rhythm of water
A definitive silence is sirens
Alternating (underneath and between)
The composition of sustenance sustained
   is stopped
The soft breath of mirrors in empty places
Caw Caw of birds at steep dawn
jerked open flower
Memory inadequate reproductions
   of stopped
Photographer stopping
Ants buried in their homes
are stopped

EPISTROPHE

LeRoi Jones

It's such a static reference; looking
out the window all the time! the eyes' limits . . .
On good days, the sun.

& what you see. (here in New York)
Walls and buildings; or in the hidden gardens
of opulent Queens: profusion, endless stretches of leisure.

It's like being chained to some dead actress;
& she keeps trying to tell you something horribly maudlin.

e.g. ("the leaves are flat & motionless.")

What I know of the mind
seems to end here;
Just outside my face.

I wish some weird looking animal
would come along.

EACH MORNING
(SECTION 4 FROM "HYMN FOR LANIE POO")

LeRoi Jones

Each morning
I go down
to Gansevoort St.
and stand on the docks.
I stare out
at the horizon
until it gets up
and comes to embrace
me. I
make believe
it is my father.
This is known
as genealogy.

DREAM

Solomon Edwards

On a straw-colored day
Came Nooney the hack
Seeking fares
In his straw hat.

Many people going places
Circle backward in their routes
Magnetized by Nooney's smile
In their wake.

Some ride ants and salamanders
Others speed at ease in clouds
Nooney fills his hat with water
Offers to a limping camel
Here the people rush and stumble
Make a sea of mud.

SKETCHES OF HARLEM

David Henderson

It was Tiny's habit
To go down to the GREAT WHITE WAY
Without understanding the subway ride.

2

The man asked Bubba to sign
A petition for more fallout shelters.
All Bubba wanted to know was
Which way the bomb was coming—
From Washington Heights
Or Sutton Place.

3

The boy arrived from Mississippi
And got a room on Seventh Avenue the same day.
Right away he wrote to Mama:
   "Dear Ma,
               I got up here safely.
   I got me a room in Harlem
   and everything is all right."

4

Black small boy asking Mama
Why the sun shines at night
And she answering that it
Ain't shining at all.
"That's a moon."

SHRINE TO WHAT SHOULD BE

Mari Evans

Come . . . have do with dillying
Let us sing a song of nobility
an ode to Righteousness
Let the children bring branches of
Trust and the women
their Dreams (no seconds nor shattered
ones please)
And the old men their constancy
and let Hope and Faith and
Charity draw near (piously please)
while we lay this wreath
of empty hearts and withered
on the shrine to
What Should Be. . . .
Quick . . . stand aᵗ attention
ignore the dirge
the insistent crescendo
of tears
falling steadily as
a soft sad black rain
from
. . . What Is
onto the shrine
of
. . . What Should Be

MADNESS ONE MONDAY EVENING

Julia Fields

Late that mad Monday evening
I made mermaids come from the sea
As the block sky sat
Upon the waves
And night came
Creeping up to me

      (I tell you I made mermaids
      Come from the sea)

The green waves lulled and rolled
As I sat by the locust tree
And the bright glare of the neon world
Sent gas-words bursting free—
Their spewed splendor fell on the billows
And gaudy it grew to me
As I sat up upon the shore
And made mermaids come from the sea.

... AND THE OLD WOMEN GATHERED

GATHERED

(THE GOSPEL SINGERS)

Mari Evans

and the old women gathered
and sang His praises
standing
resolutely together
like supply sergeants who
have seen
everything
and are still
Regular Army: It
was fierce and
not melodic and
although we ran
the sound of it
stayed in our ears ...

COME VISIT MY GARDEN

Tom Dent

Beetles,
noisy bumble bees
and yellow jackets too,
rest,
rest awhile.

Come visit my garden,
come sit with me,
come drink with me,
come abide with me,
come think, talk
and relax with me
in my garden.

Look out from my cool abode
into the hot, hot day
and rest.

Come dream with me
while I surgically remove thorns
from my sweet roses.

Enjoy with me
the insulation
of my methodically erected
clean
brick walls.

Wedding Procession, from a Window

James A. Emanuel

Together, we looked down
When the young horns blared.
We saw glassed-in grins,
Flippant ribbons,
Tough tin cans,
The bridal pair.

We looked down
The corridor of the years
And saw the wreckage,
Tough little monuments
To the Paradise that seldom was.
(Yet our fingers lightly touched.)

The Two looked up.
As if from Eden
They waved. Our hands remembered.
And the tough, young horns
Blared flippantly
Farewell.

SHOPLIFTER

Solomon Edwards

Revolving doors compete with sales-day traffic
Eject a girl who fronts a badge's glitter,
Demurs, and trips—and down some brooches clatter;
The instant people hedge this startled maverick.

Hysterics tense an incandescent hussy
Who shovels clear her lungs in septic paean;
The crowd, the cop, the caught seem posed in neon
To signal law remove an act so brassy.

Is this a girl who kindles midnight brawls,
Who sways a flood of hot intolerant blood
And cartwheels minds which bid us act insanely?

A siren whets a thief's industrious pulse.
A wagon bends its angles through a crowd
Which points a scream, a face—a face—*alone*.

THE .38

Ted Joans

I hear the man downstairs slapping the hell out of his stupid wife
    again
I hear him push and shove her around the overcrowded room
I hear his wife scream and beg for mercy
I hear him tell her there is no mercy
I hear the blows as they land on her beautiful body
I hear glasses and pots and pans falling
I hear her fleeing from the room
I hear them running up the stairs
I hear her outside my door
I hear him coming toward her outside my door
I hear her banging on my door
I hear him bang her head on my door
I hear him trying to drag her away from my door
I hear her hands desperate on my doorknob
I hear the blows of her head against my door
I hear him drag her down the stairs
I hear her head bounce from step to step
I hear them again in their room
I hear a loud smack across her face (I guess)
I hear her groan—then
I hear the eerie silence
I hear him open the top drawer of his bureau (the .38 lives there)
I hear the fast beat of my heart
I hear the drops of perspiration fall from my brow
I hear him yell I warned you
I hear him say damn you I warned you and now it's too late
I hear the loud report of the thirty eight caliber revolver then
I hear it again and again the Smith and Wesson
I hear the bang bang bang of four death dealing bullets
I hear my heart beat faster and louder—then again
I hear the eerie silence
I hear him walk out of their overcrowded room

I hear him walk up the steps
I hear him come toward my door
I hear his hand on the doorknob
I hear the doorknob click
I hear the door slowly open
I hear him step into my room
I hear the click of the thirty eight before the firing pin hits the
      bullet
I hear the loud blast of the powder exploding in the chamber
      of the .38
I hear the heavy lead nose of the bullet swiftly cutting its way
      through the barrel of the .38
I hear it emerge into space from the .38
I hear the bullet of death flying toward my head the .38
I hear it coming faster than sound the .38
I hear it coming closer to my sweaty forehead the .38
I hear its weird whistle the .38
I hear it give off a steamlike noise when it cuts through my sweat
      the .38
I hear it singe my skin as it enters my head the .38 and
I hear death saying, *Hello, I'm here!*

INSTANTANEOUS

Vivian Ayers

Instantaneously!
I was stunned . . . by a bolt
of cross-firing energies . . . more
dazzling than the Earthen Sun
. . . caught up in a blaze
resonant as a million hallelujas—
I, and all the world, were consumed
And the man within me
Died . . .
Faintly gasping,
"My god—this is GOD . . ."

HABANA

Julian Bond

Soldiers fuzz the city in khaki confusion
Pincushioned with weapons
Seedy orange venders squeeze among the pulpy masses
Camera pregnant tourists click down the Prado
Lotería salesmen tear along the dotted line
Guitars pluck loafers into corner bars
Uniformed schoolgirls genuflect languorously
Climactic roaming rainbow dresses cling slowly
Punctuating neon orgasms in the mambo night
and above Fidel's sandpaper voice,
"You want a girl, maybe?"

THE BEAST WITH CHROME TEETH

Thurmond Snyder

Make way for the beast with chrome teeth,
The glutton
Who sucks the blood of insincerity from split-level hearts.

The beast with chrome teeth,
Who sacrifices phony bodies on altars of conformity.

The beast with chrome teeth,
Who rapes the adolescent mind leaving it vacant.

The beast with chrome teeth,
Flogging bodies that are bathing in sound.
The maddening shriek of flutes,
Guttural voices of brass smashing against naked bodies
Pushing them into other dimensions.

The beast with chrome teeth,
Whose yellow tongue pushes eerie sounds out of a cavern of lies.

The beast with chrome teeth,
Whose body is covered with wounds that drop flattery's black
    dung
On white sand.

The beast with chrome teeth,
Whose bloody hands grope about the lion's mouth searching for
    success.

SEEDS

Thurmond Snyder

I stepped on the black winter seeds
Expecting a burst of violent color
To splatter over the frozen path,
But their ripeness lied to me.

They yielded a hard core.

Again I trampled the black seeds,
Grinding them underfoot,
But they were dry—there was no sign of life.

Then I wondered how these fat round
Seeds that once had sucked the sweet
Breast of nature could become
So fat and so dead.

I became frightened, I had to destroy the ugly seeds.

Again, again, and again my foot descended upon the black seeds;
But the wind came, the frightened seeds scurried about seeking
Some haven from my violence.

Some disappeared among crevices in the path,
While others took refuge
In the brown stubble of grass
That shrouded the dead park.

Then bewildered, I turned and fled the grave of seeds,
The pain in my brain was a living thing,
I had to kill it with city aspirin.
And there I brooded the winter city days away,
Unconscious of time.

Spring came!

Again I walked along the path of black seeds;
Tiny buds had sprung up among the weeds.

REVIEW FROM STATEN ISLAND

G. C. Oden

The skyline of New York does not excite me
(ferrying towards it) as mountains do in snow-steeped
                              hostility to sun.
There is something in the view—spewed up from water
                              to pure abandonment in air—
                              that snakes my spine with cold
and mouse-tracks over my heart.

Strewn across the meet of wave and wind, it seems
the incompleted play of some helter-skeltering child whose
                              hegira (as all
our circles go) has not yet led him back, but will, ripe
                              with that ferocious glee which
                              can boot these building-blocks
to earth, then heel under.

One gets used to dying living. Growth is an
end to many things—even the rose disposes of summer—
                              but still I
wince at being there when the relentless foot kicks down;
                              and the tides come roaring over
                              to pool within
the unlearned depths of me.

A PRIVATE LETTER TO BRAZIL

G. C. Oden

The map shows me where it is you are. I
am here, where the words NEW YORK run an inch
out to sea, ending where GULF STREAM flows by.

The coastline bristles with place names. The pinch
in printing space has launched them offshore
with the fish-bone's fine-tooth spread, to clinch

their urban identity. Much more
noticeable it is in the chain
of hopscotching islands that, loosely, moors

your continent to mine. (Already plain
is its eastward drift, and who could say
what would become of it left free!) Again,

the needle-pine alignment round SA,
while where it is you are (or often go),
RIO, spills its subtle phonic bouquet

Farthest seaward of all. Out there I know
the sounding is some deep 2000 feet,
and the nationalized current tours so

pregnant with resacas. In their flux meets
all the subtlety of God's great nature
and man's terse grief. See, Hero, at your feet

is not that slight tossing dead Leander?

V

IF THE STARS SHOULD FALL

Samuel Allen

Again the day
The low bleak day of the stricken years
And now the years.

The huge slow grief drives on
And I wonder why
And I grow cold
And care less
And less and less I care.

If the stars should fall,
I grant them privilege;
Or if the stars should rise to a brighter flame
The mighty dog, the buckled Orion
To excellent purposes appear to gain—
I should renew their privilege
To fall down.

It is all to me the same
The same to me
I say the great Gods, all of them,
All—cold, pitiless——
Let them fall down
Let them buckle and drop.

PREFACE TO A TWENTY VOLUME
SUICIDE NOTE

LeRoi Jones

Lately, I've become accustomed to the way
The ground opens up and envelops me
Each time I go out to walk the dog.
Or the broad edged silly music the wind
Makes when I run for a bus—

Things have come to that.

And now, each night I count the stars,
And each night I get the same number.
And when they will not come to be counted
I count the holes they leave.

Nobody sings anymore.

And then last night, I tiptoed up
To my daughter's room and heard her
Talking to someone, and when I opened
The door, there was no one there . . .
Only she on her knees,
Peeking into her own clasped hands.

THE VOYAGE OF JIMMY POO

James A. Emanuel

A soapship went a-rocking
Upon a bathtub sea.
The sailor crouched a-smiling
Upon a dimpled knee.

Young Neptune dashed the waters
Against the enamel shore,
And kept the air a-tumbling
With bubble-clouds galore.

But soon the voyage ended,
The ship was swept away
By a hand that seemed to whisper,
"No more games today."

The ship lay dry and stranded
On a shiny metal tray,
And a voice was giving orders
That a sailor must obey.

Oh, captain, little captain,
Make room for just one more
The next time you go sailing
Beyond the enamel shore.

REFLECTIONS

Carl Gardner

I saw myself leaving
And welcomed myself back
In the mirrors, I ran by too fast,
And had to retrace, to see.
I have watched myself too much
In the polished hubcaps,
Found myself smiling
Too widely in the window glass.
I stood on the corner, a statue.
Phidias would have been proud.
Too far was I leaning
Over the puddle in its peace.
I have been too witty,
Heard too much applause,
Become too wise, too full of knowing.
My chest has caught fire with the medals
For the good that I have done.
I have ordered too many executions.

DOWNTOWN-BOY UPTOWN

David Henderson

Downtown-boy uptown
Affecting complicity of a ghetto
And a sub-renascent culture.
Uptown-boy uptown for graces loomed to love.

Long have I walked these de-eternal streets
Seeking a suffix or a number to start my count.
Cat-Walk
Delicate pelican manner
Trampling the Trapezium to tapering hourglass
Behind the melting Sun.

I loved a girl then.
My 140th St. gait varied from my downtown one.
I changed my speed and form for lack of a better tongue.
Then was, love you, Pudgy:
Thin young woman with a fat black name.
It is the nature of our paradox that has us
Look to the wrong convex.

2

I stand in my low east window looking down.
Am I in the wrong slum?
The sky appears the same;
Birds fly, planes fly, clouds puff, days go . . .
I stand in my window.
Can I ride from a de-eternal genesis?
Does my exit defy concentric fish-womb?
Pudgy! your Mama always said Black man
Must stay in his balancing cup.

99

Roach on kneebone I always agreed.
Was this Black man's smile enjoying guilt
Like ofay?
> Long has it been that I've mirrored
> My entrances through silk-screen.

3

Did this tragedian kiss you in anticipation
Of blood-gush separating from your black mirror?
Did I, in my complicity-grope relay the love
Of a long gone epoch?
> Sometimes questions are not questions
If I desire to thrust once more, if I scamper to embrace
Our tragedy in my oblique arms! . . .
> Nevermind.
You know.
You are not stupid, Pudgy.
You look for nothing of a sun where you live,
Hourglass is intrinsic . . . where you live.
The regeneration in your womb is not of my body.
You have started your count.
I cannot.

THE DISTANT DRUM

Calvin C. Hernton

I am not a metaphor or symbol.
This you hear is not the wind in the trees,
Nor a cat being maimed in the street.
I am being maimed in the street.
It is I who weep, laugh, feel pain or joy,
Speak this because I exist.
This is my voice.
These words are my words,
My mouth speaks them,
My hand writes—
I am a poet.
It is my fist you hear
Beating against your ear.

MADHOUSE

Calvin C. Hernton

Here is a place that is no place
And here is no place that is a place
A place somewhere beyond the reaches of time
And beyond the reaches of those who in time
Bring flowers and fruit to this place,
Yet here is a definite place
And a definite time, fixed
In a timelessness of precise vantage
From which to view flowers and view fruit
And those who come bearing them.

Those who come by Sunday's habit are weary
And kiss us half-foreign but sympathetic,
Spread and eat noisily to crack the unbearable
Silence of this place:
They do not know that something must always come
From something and that nothing must come always
From nothing, and that nothing is always a thing

To drive us mad.

AM DRIVEN MAD

Allen Polite

I am driven mad with the printed word
The family griefs and talking to salted birds
The encoupled hours together
The assaulting reasons
The crosseyed split tongue weather
Life's old song
The peoples' heart lost
Power and treason
Joys I did not write
Sun singing in open air
A possible calm and prayerful encloaked night
A high rushing tide of dark hair

WORDS

Helen Morgan Brooks

I have forgotten you as one forgets at dawning,
The graying light, the thousand voices multiplied
From earth to sky; with all awakening things
The whole world stirs, to live again another day—
But I make bold to say, "I can forget the dawn and you."

I have forgotten you as one forgets at noon
The whitest light—the sun high in the heavens,
The heat of day, the whistles from the river barge,
The whole world stops, to rest—to nap—to play.
Still I contend, I can forget the noon and you.

I have forgotten you as one forgets at evening time—
The purple light. The shadows deep within the valley.
The softening time—when cares are not so real—
The whole world sighs and hope renewed, there's still
    another day.
Yet I know I can forget when shadows fall, you and
    the night.

I have forgotten you. This is my matin and my evensong.
I am forever busy with a thousand tasks.
Even tho, I must remember this, I have forgotten you.

WHERE HAVE YOU GONE . . .?

Mari Evans

where have you gone . . .

with your confident
walk . . . with
your crooked smile . .

why did you leave
me
when you took your
laughter
and departed
Are you aware that
with you
went the sun
all light
and what few stars
there were . . . ?

where have you gone
with your confident
walk your
crooked smile the
rent money
in one pocket and
my heart
in
another . . . .

PIROUETTE

Audre Lorde

I saw
Your hands on my lips like blind needles
Blunted
From sewing up stone
And
     Where are you from
                    you said
Your hands reading over my lips for
Some road through uncertain night
For your feet to examine home
Where are you from
                    your hands
On my lips like thunder
Promising rain;
A land where all lovers are mute.
And
     Why are you weeping
                    you said
Your hands on my doorway like rainbows
Why are you weeping?

I cannot return.

FOUR SHEETS TO THE WIND
AND A ONE-WAY TICKET TO FRANCE

Conrad Kent Rivers

As a child
I bought a red scarf and women told me
                              how beautiful it looked.
Wandering through the sous-sols as France
                              wandered through me.

In the evenings
I would watch the funny people make love
                              the way Maupassant said.
My youth allowed me the opportunity to hear
                              all those strange
verbs conjugated in erotic affirmations. I knew love at twelve.

When Selassie went before his peers and Dillinger goofed
I read in two languages, not really caring which one
                              belonged to me.

My mother lit a candle for George, my father
                              went broke, we died.
When I felt blue, the Champs understood, and when
                              it was crowded
the alley behind Harry's New York Bar soothed
                              my restless spirit.

I liked to watch the nonconformists gaze at the paintings
along Gauguin's bewildered paradise.

Braque once passed me in front of the Cafe Musique.
I used to watch those sneaky professors examine the populace.
Americans never quite fitted in, but they tried so we smiled.

I guess the money was too much for my folks.
Hitler was such a prig and a scare, we caught the long boat.
I stayed.

Main Street was never the same. I read Gide and tried to
translate Proust. Now nothing is real except French wine.
For absurdity is reality, my loneliness unreal, my mind tired.

And I shall die an old Parisian.

PLANS

Helen Morgan Brooks

My sister and I—
we've said this before—
will build a new house,
and she'll plan the door.

I know what she wants
for I know her you see:
no fancy doodads
or frail filigree.

A stout oaken door
perhaps painted white,
a wrought iron knocker,
with a chain for the night.

But me, now,
without any talent or flair,
I'm equally determined
to work on the stair.

A gay spiral stairway
I've planned so it seems
with bottom steps wide,
where children have dreams.

Then midway between
the bottom and top
a broad sort of landing
where old folk may stop.

And brides, laughingly
ascending this way
may pause and look back
to toss their bouquet.

I HEARD A YOUNG MAN SAYING

Julia Fields

I heard a young man saying
In the green afternoon,
In the sun-swept afternoon
In the bees drone afternoon,
In the peaceful, splendid afternoon,

"—War—
There's talk of war
Another decade. Another war.
One grown-up generation toward war.
Somehow, I planned on living.
What was the matter with me?
War. There's talk of war."

I, a woman, listened by the door,
By the broken-hinged door,
"I somehow planned on living."

Something plans these things.
The echo of the innocent words
Squirmed after me down the stairs,
Something plans these things . . .

TWO POEMS

Robert J. Abrams

I

I do not want to turn away
from the evening call and the
hearth's side
the warming caress of the moment sped
but
the Spring is blood this year
and the budding leaves
stab mercilessly in my heart

II

For my unborn son:
there will be no drums
no fifes—no martial music

There will be no terror
of the human insolence, no fear
of the massed savagery—the claiming hates

There will be no questions why
no queries where
no wonder when

There will be no oughts
no inevitables, no net drawn
tighter—ever tighter

There will be no God
no thee, no me, no here,
no there, no now, no then

111

There will be no lapping
of the river tongues against
the shore mouthed myrtle

There will be no bark-split awakening
no quivered silk
of willowed April

There will be no sunlight
showering red and golden
cascades in October

There will be no words
                no time
                no memory.

For my unborn son:
there is only
these waters lapping inward
under the shore mouthed myrtle

There is only
this sunlight spearing
coved shadows of raped magnolias

There is only
this flicked fear
tossed upon the waves of a moment's fury—
the swift rushing like gulls wings
and then the silent beaches.

WHEN I AWOKE

Raymond Patterson

When I awoke, she said:
Lie still, do not move.
They are all dead,
She said.

Who?
I said.

The world,
She said.

I had better go,
I said.

Why?
She said,
What good
Will it do?

I have to see,
I said.

THE PALE BLUE CASKET

Oliver Pitcher

Why don't we rock the casket here in the moonlight?

A man begins in the cradle and ends in the casket.
That's if he's a two time winner. In between? The
echo of a long lament. A mosaic of sleep. A marble
laugh. A few grapes. A short wail from the other
shore. The scattered moldy crumbs of best intentions
and the insecure peace of distance. The moon and
the sun go on playing an eternal game Show-me-yours
and I'll-show-you-mine but words fail us. We say,
here lies a man in a telephone booth, already cold
and without direct communication to the moon to
warm himself. And rock so soon!

Rock, rock, rock the casket here in the moonlight.

RAISON d'ETRE

Oliver Pitcher

Over the eye behind the moon's cloud
over you whose touch to a Stradivari heart shames
the chorale of angels
over Mr. Eros who tramples the sun-roses
and sits amid willow trees
to weep
over the olive wood
over the vibrant reds, blacks, luminous golds of
decay
over the strength of silence and advantages of
unawareness
over the Rosy Eclipse
over the geyser in the toilet bowl
over the cynical comma
over madness itself
the occupational hazard of artists
over the catcher caught in his catcher's mitt
over oil and opal, blood and bone of
the earth
over the iron touch behind pink gloves
over retired civilizations sunken below levels
shimmering in rusty lustre
over myself
I wave the flag *raison d'être.*

BIOGRAPHICAL NOTES

ROBERT J. ABRAMS, born in Philadelphia, March 1924, now lives in Brooklyn. He has a deep interest in the folk arts of the Negro people and has formed a company called Benin, Inc., to bring those arts to the American theatre and concert hall. A graphic artist holding a M.F.A. degree from Catholic University, Washington, his varied career has ranged from sales manager of a Wall Street brokerage firm to program director of a community settlement house. A very sensitive observer of life with a deep interest in metaphysics, Robert Abrams has kept an account of personal impressions and experiences since early childhood which he sometime plans to weave into a book.

SAMUEL ALLEN was born in Columbus, Ohio. Following his college years as a student of creative writing under James Weldon Johnson at Fisk University, he enrolled at the Harvard Law School, and later studied at the Sorbonne in Paris. There the late Richard Wright was instrumental in having Allen's poems published in *Presence Africaine* and for the same magazine, Allen translated into English Sartre's *Black Orpheus*. While doing his army service in Europe, he published his first book of poems, *Elfenbeinzaehne* (Ivory Tusks), in a bilingual version in Heidelberg, Germany, under the pseudonym of Paul Vesey. He has travelled widely in Africa and Latin America, and is currently Assistant General Counsel in the Legal Department of the United States Information Agency in Washington.

VIVIAN AYERS was born in Chester, South Carolina, the daughter of a blacksmith. She attended Barber-Scotia College in Concord and was graduated from Bennett College in Greensboro where her major interests were drama, music, and the dance. She has taught English at the University of Houston. Her published work includes a volume of poems, *Spice of Dawns,* and an allegorical drama of freedom and the space age, *Hawk,* which was performed on the University of Houston Educational Television Station, as well as on stage there. She spent a year in Mexico and members of the Ballet Nacional of Mexico appeared in her musical tragi-comedy, *Bow Boly.* Mrs. Ayers, with her three children, resides in Houston where she edits a quarterly publication, *Adept,* described on the masthead as being "devoted to subjects of universal human interest."

LERONE BENNETT, JR., is a graduate of Morehouse College. He lives in Chicago where he is a Senior Editor of the popular pictorial magazine, *Ebony,* and the author of an illustrated history of the Negro, *Before the Mayflower.*

JULIAN BOND (Horace Julian Bond) was born in Nashville, Tennessee, in 1940. His father, Horace Mann Bond, former president of Lincoln University (Pennsylvania), is a distinguished educational authority now on the staff of Atlanta University. Julian attended Morehouse College in Atlanta, worked on the *Atlanta Inquirer,* and is now an executive of the Student Nonviolent Coordinating Committee active in working for integration throughout the South.

HELEN MORGAN BROOKS was born in Redding, Pennsylvania, of a Quaker family. She is a graduate of St. Augustine's College in Raleigh, North Carolina, and has spent some time in study at Pendle Hill, a Quaker center in Wallingford, Pennsylvania. She is a teacher in the public schools of Philadelphia. Poetry, she says, was her first love and she began composing verses as a small child. She has contributed to various anthologies of the Delaware Poetry Society of which she is a member, has published two volumes of poems, *From These My Years* and *Against Whatever Sky,* and is an editor of the poetry magazine, *Approach.*

ISABELLA MARIA BROWN of Natchez, Mississippi, is a former teacher who lived for a time in Chicago, but has returned to Natchez where she is now a beautician, a housewife, and mother of two sons, one of whom is in the Navy. As a girl she saw the famous Rhythm Club fire in Natchez and has never forgotten the horror of it. She came from a large family of nine brothers and sisters, was tutored at home as a child, and began studying piano at the age of six. She composes the words and music of songs as well as writing poetry and fascinating letters to friends all over the country.

MARGARET DANNER was born in Kentucky but spent most of her married life in Chicago where she was an assistant editor of *Poetry*. Her poems have brought her numerous awards and a John Hay Whitney Fellowship. She has been Poet-In-Residence at Wayne University in Detroit and now lives in that city where her home, Boone House, is a center for artists and writers. In 1963 a book of her poems, *To Flower,* appeared and a recording of her poems has recently been issued by Motown Records.

TOM DENT (Thomas C. Dent), son of the president of Dillard University in New Orleans, was born in that city, but graduated from Morehouse College in Atlanta. He is the founder and editor of the Greenwich Village poetry quarterly, *Umbra*. He lives in New York City where he has recently been in charge of public relations for the Legal Defense Fund of the National Association for the Advancement of Colored People.

RAY DUREM was born in Seattle, Washington. At the age of 14 he ran away from home to join the Navy and later became a member of the International Brigades during the Civil War in Spain. In recent years he lived with his wife and daughters in Guadalajara, Mexico, where he operated a guest house. Taken with a lingering illness, he came to California for treatments and died in Los Angeles in December, 1963. His poems have been translated and anthologized in Europe as well as appearing in various collections in the United States.

SOLOMAN EDWARDS was born in 1932 in Indianapolis and is a graduate of Indiana University where in 1953 he received the Indiana University Writers Conference Poetry Award. He has taken courses at Marian College and New York University, and has studied under Louise Bogan, John Malcolm Brinnin, Richard Wilbur, and Samuel Yellen. His poems have appeared in *Voices* and *Cornucopia,* and he has recited poetry to jazz with the Dave Baker Quartet.

JAMES A. EMANUEL, born in Nebraska, was in his youth a cowboy. After serving in the armed forces in the Philippines, he studied at Howard and Northwestern Universities and is now an instructor in the Department of English at the City College of New York. He lives with his wife and son in the suburb of Mount Vernon, New York. In 1962 Emanuel received the Ph. D. degree from Columbia University for his dissertation on the short stories of Langston Hughes, and is currently working on a biography of Hughes for teenagers.

MARI EVANS, born in Toledo, Ohio, studied fashion design. Now associate editor of an industrial magazine in Indianapolis, she composes songs as well as poems, plays both piano and organ, and is a choir director. She has two sons. Her favorite sport is tennis.

JULIA FIELDS was born in Bessemer, Alabama. A graduate of Knoxville College in Tennessee, she has lived in New York, been in residence at the Bread Loaf Writers Conference in New England, and studied for a summer in Scotland. She now teaches English in a Birmingham high school and gives occasional readings of her poetry.

CARL GARDNER was born in 1931 in Washington, D.C., where he still lives. After his military service in the Air Force, he received a Bachelor of Arts degree from Howard University and is now in the Graduate School there. He writes poetry, short stories, and plays while at the same time working toward the completion of a novel.

DAVID HENDERSON, who has just turned twenty-one, was born in New York City and studied writing at the New School for Social Research there. His poems have been published in *Umbra,*

BIOGRAPHICAL NOTES

the *Seventh Street Quarterly,* and *The Black American.* He is currently at work on his first novel and sometimes appears as an actor in little theatre groups.

CALVIN C. HERNTON comes from Chattanooga, Tennessee. He studied at Talladega College and Fisk University in Nashville. He has taught English at various Southern colleges, including Edward Waters College in Jacksonville where two of his plays were produced on campus. He is now living and writing in New York while seeking publication of a first novel, and acting as one of the editors of the poetry magazine *Umbra.*

VILMA HOWARD, whose poetry has appeared in *Phylon* and the *Paris Review,* is a born New Yorker who, after her marriage to a young Englishman, now lives in Lexham Gardens, London, but frequently travels on the continent. She is a graduate of Fisk University, has one child, and sometimes works as a free lance journalist.

TED JOANS, whose father was an entertainer on Mississippi riverboats, was born on such a boat at Cairo, Illinois, on the fourth of July, 1928. Early in life he played a trumpet and has had a long-time interest in jazz, which helped to form the style of his poetry. From New York's Greenwich Village, where he was hailed both as a talented painter and a "beatnik" poet, Joans moved to Tangiers and married a Norwegian girl in Morocco where he continues to write and paint. He often travels to such romantic places as Timbuctoo for inspiration. His baby son is named Patrice Lumumba Joans. Ted has published two books of poems, *Beat* and *All of Ted Joans,* as well as a humorous pictorial, *The Hipsters,* satirizing the Beat Generation.

DON ALLEN JOHNSON, who has recently decided to use the pen name, Mustafa, for his poetry, was born in Chattanooga, Tennessee, in 1942. During his childhood his parents moved to Cleveland, Ohio, where he now lives after briefly attending Central State College in Wilberforce. There several of his poems were published in the campus newspaper. Without completing college, Johnson quit the campus for what he terms "a philo-sophical quest for certainty" which has lately taken him travelling throughout the United States.

LeROI JONES was born in Newark, New Jersey, in 1934. He studied at Howard University, Columbia University, and the New School for Social Research in New York. His service in the Air Force carried him to Puerto Rico, Europe, Africa, and the Middle East. He is editor of the avant-garde magazine, *Yungen,* and former co-editor of the mimeographed publication, *The Floating Bear,* in Greenwich Village, and a writer on jazz for *Downbeat, Metronome, Jazz,* and the *Jazz Review.* His work has also appeared in *Poetry, The Saturday Review, The Nation,* and *The Evergreen Review.* He has published a book of poems, *Preface to a Twenty Volume Suicide Note,* and a study of Negro music in America, *Blues People,* and is the author of several plays. He teaches creative writing at the New School while completing a study of the contemporary Negro intellectual in America.

OLIVER LaGRONE, as well as being a poet, is a distinguished sculptor. He was born in McAlester, Oklahoma, attended Howard University, the University of New Mexico, and the Cranbrook Art Academy in Michigan. He teaches art in the Detroit public schools where his first book of poems, *Footfalls,* was published. His latest publication is *They Speak of Dawns, A Duo-Poem Written for the Centennial Year of the Emancipation Proclamation.*

AUDRE LORDE attended Hunter College in New York City where she was born in 1934. She studied for a time at the University of Mexico, and received a degree in library service from Columbia University. To pay for her education she did ghost writing, worked as a medical clerk, an arts and crafts supervisor, and an X-Ray technician. She now works as Young Adult Librarian in the Public Library at Mount Vernon, New York.

GEORGE LOVE was born in Charlotte, North Carolina, of a fam-ily of teachers. His father was on the staff at Tuskegee. His mother still teaches grammar school in Charlotte. George graduated from Morehouse College in Atlanta, then worked for the United States government recently in Indonesia, as did his parents. He has travelled widely in Europe and South America, and is now an art photographer in New York City and a part of a cooperative photo gallery where young photographers may exhibit.

NAOMI LONG MADGETT, born in Norfolk, is a graduate of Virginia State College and holds a Master of Arts degree from Wayne University. She now teaches English at Northwestern High School in Detroit. She is the mother of three children. Her books of poems are called *Songs to A Phantom Nightingale* and *One And The Many*.

G. C. ODEN (Gloria Catherine Oden) is a graduate of Howard University and its Law School. She has held a John Hay Whitney Fellowship for Creative Writing and been a staff member of the magazine, *Urbanite*. She signs her poems with her initials, she says, as "a way of being anonymous." Miss Oden lives in New York's Greenwich Village where she reviews books, writes poetry, occasionally reads aloud in coffee houses, and has been working on a novel. She does editorial work for the American Institute of Physics. Her poems have been published in *The Saturday Review*, *The Poetry Digest*, and *The Half Moon*.

RAYMOND RICHARD PATTERSON, a native New Yorker, received his degrees from Lincoln University (Pennsylvania) and New York University. During his undergraduate days, he received a first prize for poetry in an American College and University competition sponsored by the University of Pennsylvania Press. His poems have appeared in the English anthologies, *Sixes and Sevens* and *Beyond the Blues*, as well as in the bilingual anthology, *Zag Hoe Swart ik Was*, published in Holland. Before becoming a teacher of English in the New York public schools, he worked as a counselor of delinquent youngsters at the Youth House for Boys. In Harlem he recently organized a series of readings for young Negro poets at the Market Place Gallery.

He is married, lives on Long Island, writes short stories, and is now working on his first novel.

OLIVER PITCHER was born in Massachusetts and has studied at Bard College and the Dramatic Workshop of the New School in New York City where he formerly resided. His primary interest is in playwriting, but he has published one book of poems, *Dust of Silence,* and his poems have been included in American, English, and German anthologies. He now lives in Poughkeepsie, New York.

ALLEN POLITE was born shortly before Christmas, 1932, in Newark. He came to New York to study philosophy at Columbia University and remained there as a bookseller specializing in Oriental literature. Recently he has become a code expert at the United Nations. His poetry has appeared in *Yungen* and in the London anthology, *Sixes and Sevens.*

DUDLEY RANDALL was born in Washington, D.C., graduated from Wayne University in Detroit, and received a masters degree from the University of Michigan in library science. During World War II he served in the South Pacific. He has been librarian at Lincoln University, Missouri, and Morgan College in Baltimore. He now lives in Detroit and is employed by the Wayne County Public Library there.

CONRAD KENT RIVERS, born in 1933 in Atlantic City, was graduated from Wilberforce University. He later continued his studies at Indiana University and the Chicago Teachers College. After a term in the Armed Forces, he settled down in Chicago where he now teaches and writes. His poems have appeared in the *Kenyon Review, Antioch Review, Free Lance, Signet,* and *The Ohio Poetry Review.* His booklets of poems include *Perchance To Dream, Othello,* and *These Black Bodies and This Sunburnt Face.* He acknowledges the influences of Carl Sandburg and Langston Hughes on his work.

ALFRED B. SPELLMAN, whose father and mother were both school teachers, was born in 1935 near Elizabeth City, North

Carolina. In Washington he studied at Howard University and the Howard Law School but, preferring writing to law, he now works as manager of the paperback division of a Greenwich Village bookshop and supplements his income by writing record reviews for various jazz publications. For the Pacifica Foundation's FM radio stations, Spellman moderates taped programs, does book reviews, and reads occasional papers. He also produces a series of verse plays for radio, and is one of the music editors of *Kulchur*. His first book of poems, *The Beautiful Day and Others*, appeared in 1964.

LUCY SMITH comes from Wilmington, North Carolina, but attended Penn High School in Philadelphia where she became poetry editor of her school paper and where she still lives, working as a furrier. Her first booklet of poems is called *No Middle Ground*, and she is now compiling a second with illustrations by herself.

THURMOND L. SNYDER studied at LeMoyne College in Memphis, Tennessee, his hometown. He published his first poems in campus publications and in the *Anthology of College Poetry*. In 1961 he received first prize for poetry in the *Reader's Digest*— United Negro College Fund Creative Writing Contest, and a year later was a special awards winner in the same contest.

JAMES VAUGHN was born in Xenia, Ohio. He did his military service in the South Pacific, and received degrees in journalism and in English Literature from Ohio State University. He taught at Southern University in Louisiana and at West Virginia State College. Currently he works as an editor in a New York publishing house while writing plays and poetry.

MANCE WILLIAMS of Gary, Indiana, was Literary Editor of *The Blue and Gold*, the campus magazine at Southern University, in Louisiana, where he recently completed his studies. His main interests are philosophy, jazz, and civil rights.

JAY WRIGHT was born in Albuquerque, New Mexico in 1935, but lived most of his youth in San Pedro, California, where his father was a shipyard worker. At the age of 17 as a catcher he played baseball with the Mexicali Eagles of the Arizona-Texas League, later graduating to a Fresno team in the California League. Before being called to the Army, he majored in chemistry at the University of Mexico. After three years of military service in Germany, he began the study of comparative literature at the University of California at Berkeley where he graduated. Thinking he might enter religious work, for a time he attended Union Theological Seminary in New York, but changed to the Graduate School of Rutgers University for more studies in literature. There he is doing a thesis on Calderón while acting as a graduate assistant. Short plays by Wright have been produced by the Dramatics Department of the University of California at Berkeley.

INDEX OF NAMES

Abrams, Robert J., 111
Allen, Samuel, 18, 95
Ayers, Vivian, 85

Bennett, Lerone, Jr., 53
Bond, Julian, 67, 86
Brooks, Helen Morgan, 104, 109
Brown, Isabella, 61

Danner, Margaret, 29, 30, 31
Dent, Tom, 71, 80
Durem, Ray, 33

Edwards, Solomon, 70, 75, 82
Emanuel, James A., 21, 81, 97
Evans, Mari, 19, 22, 77, 79, 105

Fields, Julia, 78, 110

Gardner, Carl, 98

Henderson, David, 76, 99
Hernton, Calvin C., 101, 102
Howard, Vilma, 58

Joans, Ted, 34, 83

Johnson, Don, 40
Jones, LeRoi, 55, 73, 74, 96

LaGrone, Oliver, 36, 37, 38
Lorde, Audre, 20, 106
Love, George, 69

Madgett, Naomi Long, 23, 39

Oden, G. C., 47, 90, 91

Patterson, Raymond, 113
Pitcher, Oliver, 114, 115
Polite, Allen, 72, 103

Randall, Dudley, 41, 43, 59
Rivers, Conrad Kent, 42, 44, 107

Smith, Lucy, 45
Snyder, Thurmond, 54, 87, 88
Spellman, Alfred B., 57, 60

Vaughn, James, 24, 62, 63

Williams, Mance, 56, 68
Wright, Jay, 17

MIDLAND BOOKS

MB-101 THE ODES OF HORACE: A CRITICAL STUDY *Commager* $2.95

MB-102 ENVIRONMENT FOR MAN: THE NEXT FIFTY YEARS *ed. Ewald* (cl. $6.95) $2.95

MB-104 FILM MAKERS ON FILM MAKING *ed. Geduld* (cloth $6.75) $1.95

MB-106 ON PHILOSOPHICAL STYLE *Blanshard* $1.25

MB-107 OPPOSITION: A LINGUISTIC AND PSYCHOLOGICAL ANALYSIS *Ogden* (cl. $3.50s) $1.50

MB-108 THE TWICE-BORN: A STUDY OF A COMMUNITY OF HIGH-CASTE HINDUS *Carstairs* $2.65

MB-109 BOSSES IN LUSTY CHICAGO: THE STORY OF BATHHOUSE JOHN AND HINKY DINK *Wendt and Kogan* (cloth $6.95s) $2.95

MB-110 THE AMERICAN SCENE *James; ed. Edel* (cloth $6.95) $2.95

MB-111 THE CONCEPT OF IRONY: WITH CONSTANT REFERENCE TO SOCRATES *Kierkegaard; tr. Capel* $2.95

MB-113 THE ART OF WILLIAM GOLDING *Oldsey and Weintraub* $1.95

MB-114 THE SHAKESPEAREAN IMAGINATION: A CRITICAL INTRODUCTION *Holland* $2.95

MB-115 MODERN GERMAN LITERATURE: THE MAJOR FIGURES IN CONTEXT *Hatfield* $1.85

MB-117 THE SKETCHBOOK OF VILLARD DE HONNECOURT *ed. Bowie* (cloth $5.75s) $2.45

MB-118 THE BURNING FOUNTAIN: A STUDY IN THE LANGUAGE OF SYMBOLISM (NEW AND REVISED EDITION) *Wheelwright* (cloth $7.50s) $2.95

MB-119 DICKENS AND CRIME *Collins* $2.95

MB-120 THE WIDENING GYRE: CRISIS AND MASTERY IN MODERN LITERATURE *Frank* $2.65

MB-121 FIVE PLAYS BY LANGSTON HUGHES; *ed. Smalley* (cloth $$5.95s) $2.65

MB-122 METAPHOR AND REALITY *Wheelwright* (cloth $5.75s) $2.45

MB-123 THE PRESENT AGE IN BRITISH LITERATURE *Daiches* (cloth $6.75) $2.65

MB-124 CHARLES DICKENS: THE WORLD OF HIS NOVELS *Miller* $2.95

MB-125 LUCRETIUS: THE WAY THINGS ARE: THE "DE RERUM NATURA" OF TITUS LUCRETIUS CARUS *tr. Humphries* (cloth $6.50) $1.95

MB-126 JAMES JOYCE TODAY: ESSAYS ON THE MAJOR WORKS *ed. Staley* (cloth $5.00) $1.95

MB-127 SAINT JOAN OF THE STOCKYARDS *Brecht; tr. Jones* (cloth $5.45) $1.95

MB-128 SCIENCE AND INDUSTRY IN THE NINETEENTH CENTURY *Bernal* (cloth $6.50s) $2.95

MB-129 SHAKESPEARE AND THE RIVAL TRADITIONS *Harbage* $3.45

MB-130 THE WALL STREET LAWYER *Smigel* (cloth $8.50s) $2.95

MB-131 TENDER IS THE NIGHT: ESSAYS IN CRITICISM *ed. LaHood* (cloth $8.50s) $1.95

MB-132 ARISTOTLE AND THE AMERICAN INDIANS: A STUDY IN RACE PREJUDICE IN THE MODERN WORLD *Hanke* $1.95

MB-133 MANY THOUSAND GONE: THE EX-SLAVES' ACCOUNT OF THEIR BONDAGE AND FREEDOM *Nichols* $2.45

MB-134 FROM VERISMO TO EXPERIMENTALISM: ESSAYS ON THE MODERN ITALIAN NOVEL *ed. Pacifici* (cloth $7.50s) $2.95

MB-135 A MAN CALLED WHITE: THE AUTOBIOGRAPHY OF WALTER WHITE $3.25

MB-136 THE GIFT OF A COW: A TRANSLATION FROM THE HINDI NOVEL "GODAAN" *Premchand; tr. Roadarmel* (cloth $7.95) $2.50